Contents

Some words are shown in bold, **like this.**
You can find out what they mean by
looking in the glossary.

Living in a desert

Deserts are the driest places in the world. Deserts are so dry that only a few plants can grow there. Deserts look bare, but they are not as empty as they look.

This tall desert plant is a cactus.

Desert
Food Chains

Angela Royston

Raintree is an imprint of Capstone Global Library Limited, a company incorporated in England and Wales having its registered office at 7 Pilgrim Street, London, EC4V 6LB – Registered company number: 6695582

www.raintreepublishers.co.uk
myorders@raintreepublishers.co.uk

Edited by Claire Throp, Diyan Leake and Helen Cox Cannons
Designed by Joanna Malivoire and Philippa Jenkins
Original illustrations © Capstone Global Library Ltd 2014
Picture research by Elizabeth Alexander and Tracy Cummins
Production by Victoria Fitzgerald
Originated by Capstone Global Library Ltd
Printed and bound in China

ISBN 9781 4062 8420 1
18 17 16 15 14
10 9 8 7 6 5 4 3 2 1

British Library Cataloguing in Publication Data
A full catalogue record for this book is available from the British Library.

Acknowledgements
We would like to thank the following for permission to reproduce photographs: Alamy pp. 12 (© George H. Huey), 14 (© Steven Folino), 15, 25 sand cat (© mike lane), 26 (© Kevin Ebi); Corbis p. 9 (© John Cancalosi/National Geographic Society); Getty Images pp. 13 (Auscape/UIG), 22 (Rachel Carbonell); Science Source p. 17d (Nature's Images); Shutterstock pp. 1 (© welcomia), 4 (© Tom Roche), 5 (© Maxim Petrichuk), 7 (© Isabella Pfenninger), 8 (© Jason Mintzer), 10, 28 (© edella), 11a (© Janelle Lugge), 11b (© Susan Flashman), 11c (© tommaso lizzul), 16 (© Bill Perry), 17a (© mallardg500), 17b (© Rusty Dodson), 17c (© Arto Hakola), 17e (© Erni), 18 (© Michal Ninger), 19 (© James Marvin Phelps), 20 (© eClick), 21 (© Piotr Gatlik), 23a, 25 hyena (© f9photos), 23b, 25 fennec fox (© Cat Downie), 23c, 25 jerboa (© reptiles4all), 24, 25 gazelle (© Serge Vero), 25 beetle (© john michael evan potter), 25 sparrow (© francesco de marco), 25 viper (© Marek Velechovsky), 27 (© Martha Marks), 29 (© Jim Feliciano); Wikimedia Commons p. 23d, 25 lovegrass (Jan Bakker).

Cover photograph of camels in Bahrain reproduced with permission of Corbis (© SOPA RF/SOPA/Corbis).

We would like to thank Michael Bright for his invaluable help in the preparation of this book.

This lizard is at home in the desert.

Many animals live in deserts. Most hide under the ground during the day. This book looks at what these animals eat and how they survive.

Where are deserts?

This map shows where the deserts are in the world. Each desert has different plants and animals living there. The plants grow in the sand or among the stones. Some deserts have rocks, and even mountains.

Deserts are marked on the map in orange.

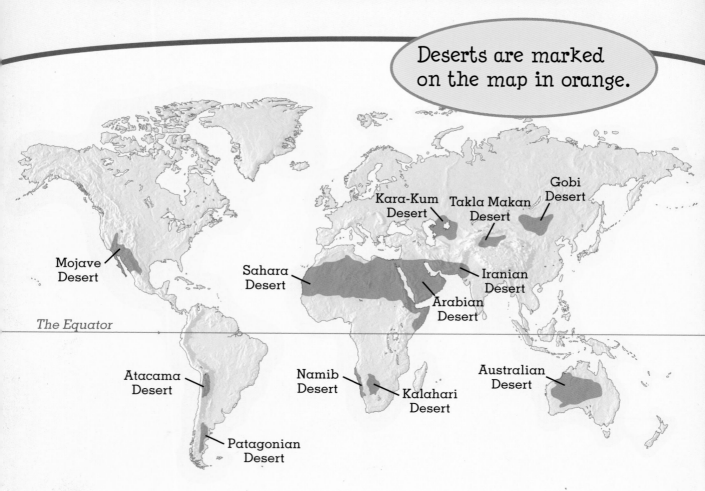

Kara-Kum Desert

Takla Makan Desert

Gobi Desert

Mojave Desert

Sahara Desert

Iranian Desert

Arabian Desert

The Equator

Atacama Desert

Namib Desert

Kalahari Desert

Australian Desert

Patagonian Desert

Sand dunes in the Sahara Desert

Largest desert

The Sahara Desert is the biggest desert in the world. Large areas of the Sahara have no plants at all.

What is a food chain?

A **food chain** shows what eats what. All living things need food, because food gives them **energy**. Living things need energy to grow and stay alive.

A roadrunner speeds across the ground looking for food.

A ground squirrel nibbles
a piece of cactus.

A food chain shows how energy in
food passes from one living thing
to another.

An Australian desert food chain

Huge lizards and small **marsupials** called bilbies form part of a **food chain** in an Australian desert. The lizard gets **energy** by eating the bilby and the bilby gets energy from eating the grass. Without the grass, both animals would not survive.

The Australian desert

Food chain

This huge lizard catches and eats the bilby

The bilby nibbles on the grass seeds

Grass grows in an Australian desert

Plants and the Sun

The lizard-bilby **food chain**, shown on page 11, begins with a plant. This is true of all desert food chains, because only plants can make their own food.

Food made in the stems of this prickly pear cactus feeds the whole plant.

Leaves produce sugar, which feeds the whole plant.

Plants are called **producers**. They produce sugary food in their leaves but they need **energy** from sunlight to do so. Plants cannot survive without the Sun.

Animal consumers

All animals are **consumers** because they find food in their environment. **Herbivores**, such as gerbils, only eat plants. They may feed on fruit, seeds, roots or leaves.

Butterflies feed on sugary nectar in flowers.

A sand cat hunts rodents and small birds.

Lizards, snakes and sand cats eat other animals. They are called **carnivores**. An **omnivore** is an animal that eats both plants and other animals.

Mojave Desert food chain

Many **food chains** have three links, but some have more. This is a food chain in the Mojave Desert. **Energy** passes from the flowers of the creosote bush to the grasshopper then on to the lizard, the snake and the hawk.

The Mojave Desert

Food chain

A hawk snatches the snake

A rattlesnake swallows the lizard

A lizard snaps up the grasshopper

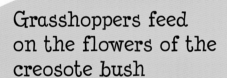

Grasshoppers feed on the flowers of the creosote bush

The creosote bush makes its own food

Top predators

A hawk is not hunted by any other animal so it is at the top of its **food chain**. Coyotes and golden eagles are also top **predators**.

This is a golden eagle.

A coyote is on the hunt for food.

It is not easy for top predators in any desert to catch food, and they need a large area to hunt in. There are fewer top predators than animals lower down the food chain.

Death and decay

Scavengers are animals that feed on the bodies of dead animals, including top predators. A vulture is a scavenger in many deserts.

Vultures feed on the flesh of dead animals.

Inside a termite nest, the insects are busy chewing up dead plants.

Some insects and bacteria are **decomposers.** They break up the remains of dead animals and plants and turn them into soil. Termites and dung beetles are decomposers.

Sahara Desert food chain

In this chain from the Sahara Desert, **energy** passes from plants to the jerboa, then to the fennec fox and on to the hyena. The hyena is a **scavenger** as well as a top **predator**.

This is the Sahara Desert.

Food chain

The hyena hunts the fennec fox

A fennec fox catches and eats the jerboa

A jerboa eats plants growing in the desert

Lovegrass grows in the Sahara Desert

Food webs

Animals have a choice of food, even in the Sahara Desert. They survive by eating a wide range of food. The diagram opposite shows how different **food chains** link together to form a **food web**.

A gazelle roams across the desert, nibbling grass and other plants.

Food web

sand cat

hyena

horned viper

fennec fox

desert sparrow

gazelle

jerboa

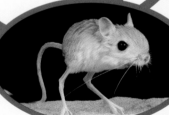

dung beetle

lovegrass

Broken chains

A break in one **food chain** can damage other food chains. For example, desert tortoises spread the seeds of the plants that they eat. This helps more plants to grow.

A tortoise snacks on a flower in the Mojave Desert.

Blacktailed jackrabbits hide in burrows made by desert tortoises.

There are now many fewer tortoises in the Mojave than there used to be. Without the tortoises there are fewer plants and animals.

Protecting food chains

People are the biggest threat to desert animals and **food chains**. For example, in the past, people brought thousands of camels to Australia. The camels escaped into the desert and now compete for food with Australian desert animals.

This wild camel is in the Australian outback.

A visitor centre for tourists in the Sonoran Desert.

Nature reserves have been set up in some deserts to protect wildlife and inform people about the plants and animals.

Glossary

carnivore animal that eats only the meat of other animals

consumer living thing, particularly an animal, that feeds on other living things, such as plants and other animals

decomposer living thing, such as an earthworm, fungus or bacterium, that breaks up the remains of plants and animals and turns them into soil

energy power needed to do something, such as move, breathe or swallow

food chain diagram that shows how energy passes from plants to different animals

food web diagram that shows how different plants and animals in a habitat are linked by what they eat

herbivore animal that eats only plants

marsupial type of mammal, such as the kangaroo or wallaby. The mother usually carries and suckles its babies in a pouch in its belly.

omnivore animal that eats plants and animals

predator animal that hunts other animals for food

producer living thing, such as a plant, that makes its own food

scavenger animal that feeds off the flesh and remains of dead animals

Find out more

Books

Desert Food Chains (Protecting Food Chains), Buffy Silverman (Raintree, 2010)

Deserts (Geographywise), Leon Gray (Wayland, 2010)

Deserts (Life Cycles), Sean Callery (Kingfisher, 2012)

Who Eats Who in the Desert? (Food Chains in Action), Andrew Campbell (Franklin Watts, 2009)

Websites

environment.nationalgeographic.com/environment/ photos/desert-wildlife
This section of the National Geographic website provides photos of different desert animals.

www.alicespringsdesertpark.com.au/kids
This website tells you about Australian deserts and has links to the Sonoran Desert, too.

www.bbc.co.uk/nature/habitats/Deserts_and_xeric_ shrublands#intro
This BBC website has video clips of amazing plants and animals from different deserts around the world.

Index